FLORIDA Bingo Book

COMPLETE BINGO GAME IN A BOOK

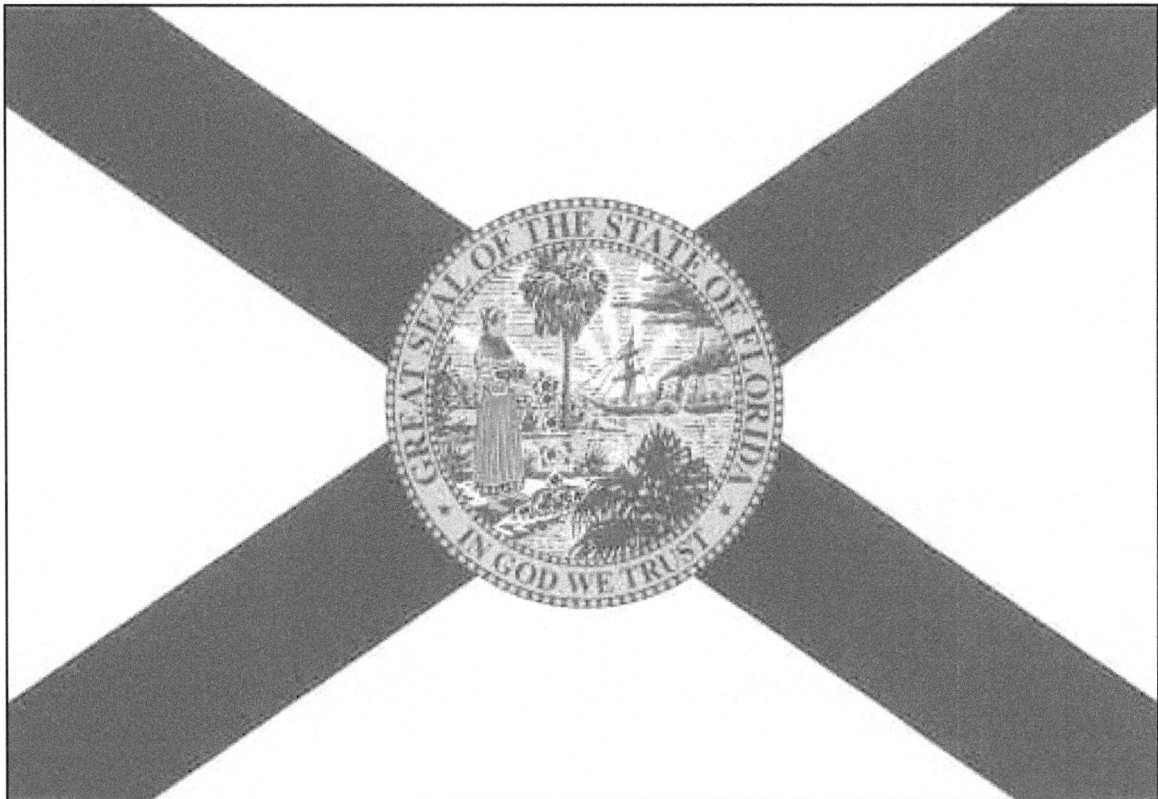

Written By Rebecca Stark

ISBN 978-0-87386-502-9

Educational Books 'n' Bingo

Printed in the U.S.A.

FLORIDA BINGO
Directions

INCLUDED:

List of Terms

Templates for Additional Terms and Clues

2 Clues per Term

30 Unique Bingo Cards

Markers

1. **Either cut apart the book or make copies of ALL the sheets. You might want to make an extra copy of the clue sheets to use for introduction and review. Keep the sheets in an envelope for easy reuse.**

2. Cut apart the call cards with terms and clues.

3. Pass out one bingo card per student. There are enough for a class of 30.

4. Pass out markers. You may cut apart the markers included in this book or use any other small items of your choice.

5. Decide whether or not you will require the entire card to be filled. Requiring the entire card to be filled provides a better review. However, if you have a short time to fill, you may prefer to have them do the just the border or some other format. Tell the class before you begin what is required.

6. There are 50 topics. Read the list before you begin. If there are any topics that have not been covered in class, you may want to read to the students the topic and clues before you begin.

7. There is a blank space in the middle of each card. You can instruct the students to use it as a free space or you can write in answers to cover topics not included. Of course, in this case you would create your own clues. (Templates provided.)

8. Shuffle the cards and place them in a pile. Two or three clues are provided for each topic. If you plan to play the game with the same group more than once, you might want to choose a different clue for each game. If not, you may choose to use more than one clue.

9. Be sure to keep the cards you have used for the present game in a separate pile. When a student calls, "Bingo," he or she will have to verify that the correct answers are on his or her card AND that the markers were placed in response to the proper questions. Pull out the cards that are on the student's card keeping them in the order they were used in the game. Read each clue as it was given and ask the student to identify the correct answer from his or her card.

10. If the student has the correct answers on the card AND has shown that they were marked in response to the *correct questions,* then that student is the winner and the game is over. If the student does not have the correct answers on the card OR he or she marked the answers in response to *the wrong questions,* then the game continues until there is a proper winner.

11. If you want to play again, reshuffle the cards and begin again.

Have fun!

TERMS INCLUDED

Adams-Onis Treaty	Lake(s)
Border	Legislative Branch
Cape Canaveral	Louisiana Purchase
Climate	Manatee
Coastal Plain	Miami
Coastline	Orlando
Confederacy (-ate)	Osceola
Counties	Palm Beach
Daytona	Panhandle
Ponce de Leon	Peninsula
Hernando de Soto	Pensacola
Sir Francis Drake	Henry Plant
William Duval	Orange(s)
Everglades	Population
Executive Branch	River(s)
Flag	Reptile
Henry Flagler	Seminoles
Gulf of Mexico	Seminole War(s)
Hurricane	Spain
Industry	St. Augustine
Intracoastal Waterway	Sunshine State
Andrew Jackson	Tallahassee
Jacksonville	Tampa
Judicial Branch	Union
Keys	Uplands

Additional Terms

Choose as many additional terms as you would like and write them in the squares.
Repeat each as desired.
Cut out the squares and randomly distribute them to the class.
Instruct the students to place their square on the center space of their card.

Florida Bingo

Clues for Additional Terms

Write three clues for each of your additional terms.

<table>
<tr><td>

_____

1.

2.

3.

</td><td>

_____

1.

2.

3.

</td></tr>
<tr><td>

_____

1.

2.

3.

</td><td>

_____

1.

2.

3.

</td></tr>
<tr><td>

_____

1.

2.

3.

</td><td>

_____

1.

2.

3.

</td></tr>
</table>

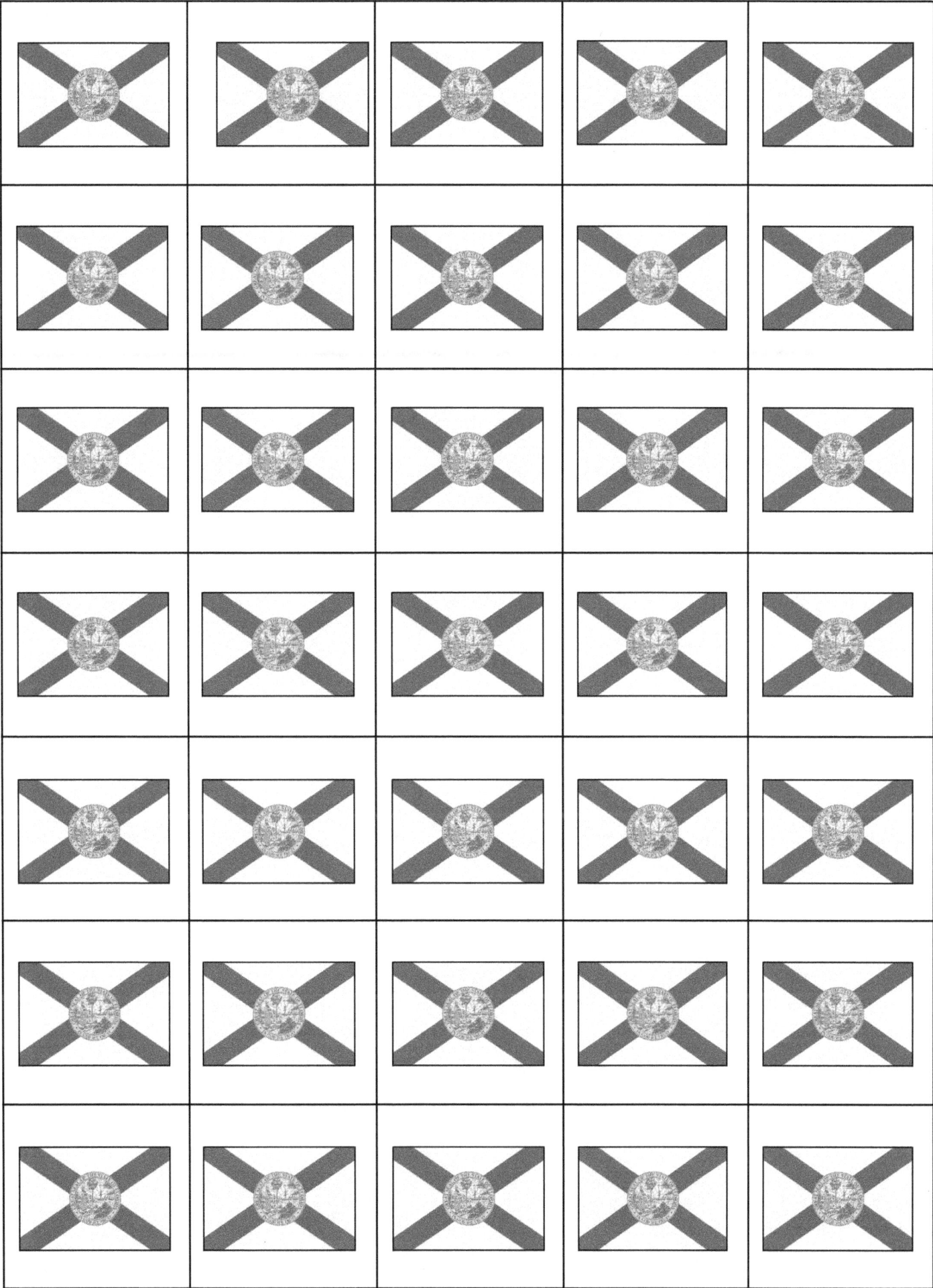

Adams-Onis Treaty
1. The United States acquired Florida from Spain in 1821 with the ___.
2. The Treaty of Acquisition, also known as the ___, between the United States and Spain gave East and West Florida to the United States.

Border
1. Georgia and Alabama are the only states that ___ Florida.
2. Two bodies of water ___ Florida: the Atlantic Ocean and the Gulf of Mexico.

Cape Canaveral
1. Several major American space exploration "firsts" were launched from the ___ Air Force Station. They include the first U.S. Earth satellite, the first U.S. astronaut, the first U.S. astronaut in orbit, and several others.
2. The Kennedy Space Center is in ___.

Climate
1. Most of Florida has a sub-tropical ___. Summers are long, warm, and fairly humid. Winters are mostly mild.
2. The ___ in the Keys is technically sub-tropical, but because they are so close to the Tropic of Cancer, they never get frost.

Coastal Plain
1. The ___ regions are characterized by low, flat land. Off the mainland are sand bars, coral reefs and barrier islands.
2. There are two ___ regions: the Atlantic ___ and the East Gulf ___.

Coastline
1. Florida has the longest ___ in the contiguous United States.
(contiguous: connecting without a break)
2. Florida's ___ is about 1,350 miles long; it is the only state to border both the Gulf of Mexico and the Atlantic Ocean.

Confederacy (-ate)
1. Florida was the third state to secede from the Union and join the ___.
2. John Milton was the governor of the ___ State of Florida.

County (-ies)
1. There are 67 ___ in Florida.
2. Miami-Dade is the ___ with the largest population.

Daytona
1. This city on the Atlantic coast is known for its automobile race track.
2. ___ is the home of the ___ 500, one of the most prestigious NASCAR races.

Ponce de Leon
1. ___ led the first European expedition to Florida. He landed on the shore of what he would name Florida in 1513.
2. Legend tells us he was searching for the Fountain of Youth, which he believed to be in Florida.

Florida Bingo

© Barbara M. Peller

Hernando de Soto 1. ___ arrived on the west coast of Florida in May 1539 with 10 ships carrying soldiers, priests, and explorers. He was influenced by the achievements of Juan Ponce de León, who had discovered Florida in 1513. 2. He was the first explorer documented to have crossed the Mississippi River.	**Sir Francis Drake** 1. In 1586 ___ and his soldiers raided the fort at St. Augustine in Spanish Florida. 2. ___ was a hero to the English, but a pirate to the Spaniards.
William Duval 1. ___ was the first civilian governor of Florida Territory. He was governor from 1822 to 1834. 2. Jacksonville is the seat of the county named for ___.	**Everglades** 1. The swampy region known as the ___ is the largest subtropical wilderness in the nation. 2. Florida's symbolic animals, including the American alligator, the Florida panther, and the manatee, can be found in the ___.
Executive Branch 1. In addition to the governor and lieutenant governor, the ___ includes a Cabinet composed of an attorney general, a chief financial officer, and a commissioner of agriculture. 2. The governor is head of the ___. The present-day governor is [fill in].	**Flag** 1. The state ___ has 2 diagonal red bars on a white field. 2. The Great Seal is in the center of the state ___. It contains the state motto, "In God We Trust." A Seminole woman is also on the seal.
Henry Flagler 1. ___ was founder of what became the Florida East Coast Railway and a founder of Standard Oil. 2. ___ founded Palm Beach. He built a mansion named Whitehall there.	**Gulf of Mexico** 1. Tampa, Venice, Largo and Clearwater Beach are on the ___. 2. The Florida Strait is located between the ___ and the Atlantic Ocean and between the Florida Keys and Cuba.
Hurricane 1. A ___ is an intense tropical weather system of strong thunderstorms with a well-defined surface circulation and maximum sustained winds of 74 mph or higher. 2. The Atlantic ___ season is officially June 1 to November 30.	**Industry** 1. Tourism is a very important ___ in Florida. The state is one of the world's top travel destinations. 2. Agriculture is an important ___. Florida leads the southeast in farm income. Important crops include citrus fruits, sugarcane, tomatoes, and strawberries.

Intracoastal Waterway 1. The ___ is a 3,000-mile waterway along the Atlantic and Gulf coasts of the United States. 2. The ___ consists of two non-contiguous segments. The Gulf ___ and The Atlantic ___. (contiguous: connecting without a break)	**Andrew Jackson** 1. ___ led an invasion of Spanish Florida during the First Seminole War. 2. ___ was the first military governor of Florida. He would later become the seventh President of the United States.
Jacksonville 1. When the city and county government consolidated in 1968, ___ became the largest city in Florida in both land area and population. 2. This city is named after the seventh President of the United States.	**Judicial Branch** 1. The ___ interprets what our laws mean and makes decisions about the laws and those who break them. 2. It is made up of several courts, the highest of which is the state Supreme Court.
Keys 1. The Florida ___ are an archipelago. The archipelago comprises about 1,700 islands. 2. The Florida ___ extend southwest from the southeastern tip of the Florida peninsula to the uninhabited Dry Tortugas in the Gulf of Mexico.	**Lake(s)** 1. ___ Okeechobee is the state's largest inland body of water. 2. Apopka, George, Harney, Istokpoga, Kissimmee, and Okeechobee are some of Florida's ___.
Legislative Branch 1. The ___ of state government is called the General Assembly. It comprises the Senate and the House of Representatives. 2. The ___ makes the laws.	**Louisiana Purchase** 1. In 1803 the United States bought about 828,000 square miles of land from France. This is called the ___. 2. After the ___ of 1803, there were boundary disputes regarding Florida. President Jefferson argued that Florida was included in the agreement.
Manatee 1. The ___ is the official state marine mammal. Other mammals that are state symbols include the dolphin, the panther, and the Cracker horse. 2. This large, gentle, aquatic mammal is sometimes known as a sea cow.	**Miami** 1. The Port of ___ is sometimes called "The Cruise Capital of the World." 2. Julia Tuttle is sometimes called the "Mother of ___." She convinced Henry Flagler to extend his railroad to this city.

Orlando	Osceola
1. ___ is in Central Florida. It is the county seat of Orange County. 2. The Greater ___ area is best known for its theme parks, which include Walt Disney World, Universal Studios, and Sea World.	1. This Creek warrior led a band of Seminoles during the Second Seminole War. 2. The U.S. soldiers tricked ___ by pretending to want to talk peace. A county in Florida is named for him; Kissimmee is the county seat.
Palm Beach 1. Palm Beach is a barrier island sixteen miles long about 65 miles north of Miami. It was established as a resort by Henry Flagler. 2. Henry Flagler made this Atlantic coast barrier island accessible via his Florida East Coast Railway.	**Panhandle** 1. The northwestern part of the state is often called the Florida ___. Tallahassee and Pensacola are both in the ___. 2. The ___ is the informal term for the strip of land about 200 miles long and 50 to 100 miles wide in the northwestern part of the state.
Peninsula 1. A ___ is connected to a mainland on one side and bordered by water on the other three sides. 2. Most of Florida is a ___. Three sides are surrounded by the Gulf of Mexico, the Atlantic Ocean, and the Straits of Florida.	**Pensacola** 1. ___ was the capital of Spanish Florida. 2. ___ is the westernmost city in the Florida Panhandle. It is the county seat of Escambia County.
Henry Plant 1. This railroad builder helped develop Florida's west coast. A city near Tampa is named for him. 2. ___ developed a system of railroads and steamboats that helped develop the west coat.	**Orange(s)** 1. It is not surprising that the ___ is the state fruit. Citrus fruits, especially ___, are a major part of Florida's economy. 2. ___ juice is the state beverage, and the ___ blossom is the state flower.
Population 1. In 2011 the ___ of Florida was over 19 million. 2. In 2011 Florida passed New York and became the third largest state in terms of ___.	**River(s)** 1. The Apalachicola, Caloosahatchee, Indian, Kissimmee, St Johns and Suwannee are ___ in Florida. 2. The St. Johns ___ is the longest in the state.

Florida Bingo

Reptile 1. The American Alligator is the official state ___. 2. The loggerhead turtle is the official state saltwater ___.	**Seminoles** 1. Many runaway slaves joined the ___ in Spanish Florida. 2. When Florida became a territory, the ___ were ordered to leave. Many refused, and some fled to the Everglades to hide.
Seminole War(s) 1. There were three ___: 1832–1835, 1835–1842, and 1855–1858. 2. The Second ___ was the fiercest. The U.S. tried to enforce the Treaty of Payne's Landing and force the Seminoles to leave.	**Spain** 1. In 1763 ___ traded Florida to Great Britain in exchange for control of Havana, Cuba. 2. When the American Revolution ended in 1783, ___ regained control of Florida from Britain as part of the Treaty of Paris.
St. Augustine 1. ___ is the oldest continuously inhabited European settlement in the state; it is second oldest only to San Juan, Puerto Rico, in the current territory of the United States. 2. Pedro Menéndez de Avilés founded ___. It was the first successful Spanish foothold in La Florida.	**Sunshine State** 1. Florida's nickname is the "___." 2. Some license plates have the state's nickname, which is the " ___." Some have its motto, which is "In God we trust."
Tallahassee 1. ___ is the capital of the state. It is in the part of the state called the Panhandle. 2. ___ is home to several colleges and universities, including Florida State University and Florida A&M University.	**Tampa** 1. ___ is on the Gulf of Mexico in Hillsborough County. 2. Ybor City is a historic neighborhood in ___. It was founded in the 1880s by cigar manufacturers. The neighborhood has been designated as a National Historic Landmark District.
Union 1. Florida was the 27th state to join the ___. 2. Florida joined the ___ on March 3, 1845.	**Uplands** 1. The ___ start in the northwest and extend into the central area of the Florida peninsula. The geographic region is characterized by low, rolling hills of red clay. 2. Britton Hill, the state's highest point, is in this region, but it is only 345 feet above sea level. That is the lowest "highest point" of all 50 states!

Florida Bingo

© Barbara M. Peller

Florida Bingo

Orange(s)	Adams-Onis Treaty	Cape Canaveral	Hurricane	Coastal Plain
Henry Flagler	Border	Tampa	Orlando	Reptile
Tallahassee	Miami		Pensacola	Union
Sunshine State	River(s)	St. Augustine	Manatee	Palm Beach
Peninsula	Jacksonville	Everglades	Seminole War(s)	Lake(s)

Florida Bingo

Sunshine State	Tallahassee	Keys	Population	Louisiana Purchase
Palm Beach	Executive Branch	Counties	River(s)	Panhandle
Ponce de Leon	Jacksonville		Judicial Branch	St. Augustine
Henry Plant	Intracoastal Waterway	Miami	Uplands	Coastal Plain
Reptile	Tampa	Everglades	Henry Flagler	Seminole War(s)

Florida Bingo

Jacksonville	St. Augustine	Executive Branch	Manatee	Tallahassee
Palm Beach	Border	Daytona	Adams-Onis Treaty	Andrew Jackson
River(s)	Tampa		Panhandle	Climate
Miami	Ponce de Leon	Peninsula	Henry Plant	Keys
Seminole War(s)	Hernando de Soto	Everglades	Uplands	Louisiana Purchase

Florida Bingo

Miami	Panhandle	Cape Canaveral	Hernando de Soto	Louisiana Purchase
Osceola	Confederacy (-ate)	Adams-Onis Treaty	Population	Tallahassee
Pensacola	Henry Plant		Lake(s)	Hurricane
St. Augustine	Border	Tampa	Everglades	Counties
Sir Francis Drake	Reptile	Coastline	Seminole War(s)	Union

Florida Bingo

Reptile	Coastal Plain	River(s)	Counties	Hernando de Soto
Osceola	St. Augustine	Daytona	Judicial Branch	Border
Cape Canaveral	Union		Orlando	Industry
Lake(s)	Louisiana Purchase	Orange(s)	Uplands	William Duval
Executive Branch	Everglades	Tallahassee	Miami	Pensacola

Florida Bingo

Climate	Panhandle	Keys	Louisiana Purchase	Union
Manatee	River(s)	William Duval	Adams-Onis Treaty	Tallahassee
Population	Sir Francis Drake		Confederacy (-ate)	Judicial Branch
Everglades	Peninsula	Uplands	Coastline	Cape Canaveral
Palm Beach	Counties	Orange(s)	Pensacola	Flag

Florida Bingo

Orange(s)	Panhandle	Industry	St. Augustine	Executive Branch
Palm Beach	Louisiana Purchase	Jacksonville	Border	Osceola
Union	Hurricane		Judicial Branch	Confederacy (-ate)
Miami	Henry Plant	Daytona	Sunshine State	Ponce de Leon
Everglades	Hernando de Soto	Uplands	Coastline	Climate

Florida Bingo

Pensacola	Panhandle	Gulf of Mexico	Manatee	Confederacy (-ate)
Osceola	Cape Canaveral	Population	Union	Counties
Flag	Hernando de Soto		Louisiana Purchase	Coastal Plain
Seminole War(s)	Miami	Sunshine State	Sir Francis Drake	Henry Plant
Tampa	Everglades	Coastline	River(s)	Palm Beach

Florida Bingo

Judicial Branch	Executive Branch	Jacksonville	Flag	Hernando de Soto
Sir Francis Drake	Louisiana Purchase	Pensacola	River(s)	Panhandle
Andrew Jackson	Orange(s)		Border	Gulf of Mexico
William Duval	Coastal Plain	Peninsula	Orlando	Industry
Henry Plant	Uplands	Daytona	Sunshine State	Lake(s)

Florida Bingo

Sunshine State	Manatee	Confederacy (-ate)	Population	Flag
Union	Counties	Adams-Onis Treaty	Border	Louisiana Purchase
Hernando de Soto	Panhandle		Hurricane	Ponce de Leon
Peninsula	Lake(s)	William Duval	Uplands	Andrew Jackson
Daytona	Palm Beach	Keys	Reptile	Pensacola

Florida Bingo

Climate	Panhandle	River(s)	William Duval	Palm Beach
Gulf of Mexico	Andrew Jackson	Orlando	Judicial Branch	Adams-Onis Treaty
Osceola	Louisiana Purchase		Keys	Jacksonville
Daytona	Tallahassee	Uplands	Hernando de Soto	Sunshine State
Sir Francis Drake	Everglades	Orange(s)	Coastline	Executive Branch

Florida Bingo

Executive Branch	Coastal Plain	Andrew Jackson	Manatee	Judicial Branch
Jacksonville	Palm Beach	Cape Canaveral	Coastline	Border
Orange(s)	Industry		Union	Population
Everglades	Henry Plant	Louisiana Purchase	Sunshine State	Osceola
Panhandle	Gulf of Mexico	Hernando de Soto	Sir Francis Drake	Counties

Florida Bingo

William Duval	Coastal Plain	Climate	Andrew Jackson	Union
Cape Canaveral	Gulf of Mexico	Louisiana Purchase	Judicial Branch	Ponce de Leon
Manatee	Counties		Jacksonville	Industry
Pensacola	Uplands	Confederacy (-ate)	Hernando de Soto	Sunshine State
Everglades	Lake(s)	Coastline	Orange(s)	Orlando

Union	Andrew Jackson	Climate	Coastal Plain	William Duval
			Gulf of Mexico	
Orlando		Satellite		Everglades

Florida Bingo

Henry Flagler	Louisiana Purchase	River(s)	Judicial Branch	Sir Francis Drake
Counties	Orange(s)	Andrew Jackson	Border	Panhandle
William Duval	Hurricane		Keys	Daytona
Lake(s)	Uplands	Hernando de Soto	Confederacy (-ate)	Climate
Everglades	Population	Ponce de Leon	Palm Beach	Pensacola

Florida Bingo

Orlando	Judicial Branch	River(s)	Executive Branch	Manatee
Climate	Keys	Adams-Onis Treaty	Cape Canaveral	Sir Francis Drake
Union	Orange(s)		Tallahassee	Panhandle
Everglades	Andrew Jackson	Gulf of Mexico	Uplands	William Duval
Palm Beach	Henry Plant	Coastline	Flag	Jacksonville

Florida Bingo

Confederacy (-ate)	Andrew Jackson	Gulf of Mexico	Flag	Intracoastal Waterway
Population	Ponce de Leon	Industry	Osceola	Hurricane
William Duval	Coastal Plain		Union	Jacksonville
Miami	Counties	Everglades	Orlando	Sunshine State
Sir Francis Drake	Spain	Coastline	Henry Plant	Panhandle

Florida Bingo: Card No. 16

Florida Bingo

Daytona	Seminoles	Legislative Branch	Andrew Jackson	Henry Flagler
Orlando	Sir Francis Drake	Uplands	Hurricane	Industry
Judicial Branch	Pensacola		Spain	Gulf of Mexico
Lake(s)	Palm Beach	Sunshine State	River(s)	Ponce de Leon
Peninsula	William Duval	Executive Branch	Manatee	Coastal Plain

Florida Bingo

Flag	Hernando de Soto	Counties	William Duval	Population
Panhandle	Daytona	Peninsula	Union	Sir Francis Drake
Judicial Branch	Ponce de Leon		Legislative Branch	Cape Canaveral
Coastal Plain	Adams-Onis Treaty	Uplands	Sunshine State	Keys
Spain	Andrew Jackson	River(s)	Seminoles	Climate

Florida Bingo

Union	Climate	Andrew Jackson	Gulf of Mexico	Sunshine State
Orlando	Manatee	Panhandle	Executive Branch	Hurricane
Seminoles	Hernando de Soto		Border	Tallahassee
Keys	Spain	Peninsula	Henry Plant	Legislative Branch
Cape Canaveral	Intracoastal Waterway	Palm Beach	Pensacola	Coastline

Florida Bingo

Henry Flagler	Seminoles	Manatee	Andrew Jackson	Coastline
Counties	Jacksonville	Osceola	Peninsula	Population
Coastal Plain	Industry		Miami	Adams-Onis Treaty
Reptile	Tampa	Seminole War(s)	Henry Plant	Spain
St. Augustine	Pensacola	Intracoastal Waterway	Sunshine State	Legislative Branch

Florida Bingo

Orlando	Climate	Osceola	Andrew Jackson	Reptile
Coastal Plain	Legislative Branch	Confederacy (-ate)	Gulf of Mexico	Orange(s)
Ponce de Leon	Palm Beach		Seminoles	River(s)
Peninsula	Executive Branch	Spain	Lake(s)	Pensacola
Miami	Intracoastal Waterway	Coastline	Daytona	Henry Plant

Florida Bingo

Flag	Keys	Legislative Branch	Cape Canaveral	William Duval
Population	Manatee	Tallahassee	Gulf of Mexico	Border
Counties	Hurricane		Orange(s)	Industry
Spain	Lake(s)	Henry Plant	Adams-Onis Treaty	Osceola
Intracoastal Waterway	Daytona	Seminoles	Ponce de Leon	St. Augustine

Florida Bingo

Confederacy (-ate)	Seminoles	Executive Branch	Cape Canaveral	Coastline
Climate	Henry Flagler	Palm Beach	Orlando	Adams-Onis Treaty
Keys	William Duval		Seminole War(s)	Orange(s)
Ponce de Leon	Intracoastal Waterway	Spain	Daytona	Henry Plant
Reptile	Tampa	Pensacola	Peninsula	Legislative Branch

Florida Bingo

Confederacy (-ate)	Pensacola	Henry Flagler	Seminoles	Gulf of Mexico
Legislative Branch	Coastline	Osceola	Population	Orange(s)
Industry	Flag		William Duval	Ponce de Leon
Reptile	Seminole War(s)	Spain	Daytona	Coastal Plain
St. Augustine	Miami	Intracoastal Waterway	Manatee	Tampa

Florida Bingo

Miami	Osceola	Seminoles	River(s)	Legislative Branch
Adams-Onis Treaty	Coastal Plain	Orlando	Confederacy (-ate)	Border
Lake(s)	Gulf of Mexico		Seminole War(s)	Spain
Tallahassee	Reptile	Tampa	Intracoastal Waterway	Hurricane
Coastline	Henry Flagler	Counties	Sir Francis Drake	St. Augustine

Florida Bingo

Legislative Branch	Seminoles	Keys	Population	Flag
Peninsula	Manatee	Gulf of Mexico	Henry Flagler	Confederacy (-ate)
Lake(s)	Seminole War(s)		Hurricane	Miami
Daytona	Cape Canaveral	Reptile	Intracoastal Waterway	Spain
Industry	Sir Francis Drake	River(s)	Tampa	St. Augustine

Florida Bingo

Keys	Counties	Seminoles	Henry Flagler	Jacksonville
Reptile	Seminole War(s)	Orlando	Spain	Border
Uplands	Tampa		Intracoastal Waterway	Miami
Flag	Climate	Osceola	St. Augustine	Adams-Onis Treaty
Sir Francis Drake	Hurricane	Legislative Branch	Tallahassee	Industry

Florida Bingo: Card No. 27

Florida Bingo

Keys	Henry Flagler	Tallahassee	Seminoles	Confederacy (-ate)
Jacksonville	Legislative Branch	Seminole War(s)	Population	Hurricane
Tampa	Ponce de Leon		Industry	Peninsula
Sunshine State	Flag	Palm Beach	Intracoastal Waterway	Spain
Cape Canaveral	Judicial Branch	Sir Francis Drake	St. Augustine	Reptile

Florida Bingo

Legislative Branch	Henry Flagler	Flag	Orlando	Judicial Branch
Henry Plant	Peninsula	Osceola	Industry	Tallahassee
Lake(s)	Seminole War(s)		Border	Seminoles
Jacksonville	Reptile	Louisiana Purchase	Intracoastal Waterway	Spain
Confederacy (-ate)	Gulf of Mexico	St. Augustine	Climate	Tampa

Florida Bingo

Hernando de Soto	Seminoles	Population	Judicial Branch	Spain
Adams-Onis Treaty	Henry Flagler	Keys	Hurricane	Border
Lake(s)	William Duval		Industry	Osceola
St. Augustine	Climate	Cape Canaveral	Intracoastal Waterway	Seminole War(s)
Reptile	Union	Tampa	Legislative Branch	Tallahassee

www.ingramcontent.com/pod-product-compliance
Lightning Source LLC
LaVergne TN
LVHW061337060426
835511LV00014B/1975